From Average
to
EXCEPTIONAL

Adopting the Habits of
Highly Effective
People

Alberto M. Ball

Table of Contents

Introduction

In today's fast-paced world, success is often determined by the habits we cultivate and maintain. Highly effective people are those who consistently achieve their goals and lead fulfilling lives. They possess unique qualities and habits that set them apart from the average person. Here are a few things that differentiate highly effective people from others:

Clarity of purpose: Effective people have a clear understanding of what they want to achieve and why it is important to them. This clarity allows them to focus their time and energy on what truly matters, rather than being distracted by unimportant things.

Good habits: Highly effective people have developed positive habits that help them achieve their goals. This can include things like waking up early, exercising regularly, and being organized. They also avoid bad habits that can derail their progress, such as procrastination and multitasking.

Prioritization: Effective people are skilled at prioritizing their tasks and focusing on the most important ones first. This allows them to make the most of their time and ensure that they are making progress toward their goals.

Self-discipline: Highly effective people have strong self-discipline, which allows them to follow through on their commitments and stay focused on their goals, even when things get tough. They are able to resist distractions and temptations and remain committed to their plans.

Continuous learning: Effective people never stop learning. They are constantly seeking out new information and knowledge to improve themselves and their skills. This helps them to stay ahead of the curve and achieve their goals more effectively.

Positive mindset: Highly effective people have a positive mindset and are able to maintain an optimistic outlook, even in the face of challenges and setbacks. This helps them to stay motivated and focused on their goals, and it also enables them to be more resilient when things don't go according to plan.

Strong relationships: Effective people have strong relationships with others, which they cultivate through communication, empathy, and mutual support. They understand the importance of having a supportive network of friends and family, and they work to maintain those relationships.

Highly effective people possess a unique combination of qualities and habits that enable them to achieve their goals and lead fulfilling lives. By understanding and emulating these traits, anyone can become more effective and lead a more fulfilling life.

The choices we make daily have a profound impact on the direction of our lives and the achievement of our goals.

In "From Average to Exceptional", we delve into the habits of those who have achieved great success and examine the strategies they use to maintain and cultivate these habits.

Through inspiring stories, practical tips, and thought-provoking insights, this book provides a roadmap for developing and strengthening the habits that lead to a more fulfilling and successful life.

Whether you're looking to improve your health, relationships, or career, this book will give you the tools and guidance you need to make lasting changes and achieve your full potential.

Before going into the first chapter, dear reader, I want to remind you that you are indeed a powerful and unstoppable force of nature. With the right habits and mindset, you can accomplish anything you set your mind to.

To achieve your goals, it's important to focus on developing effective habits that support your growth and progress. This can include things like creating a daily routine, prioritizing self-care and rest, and making time for continuous learning and personal development.

In addition, it's crucial to adopt a growth mindset and be open to learning and evolving as you go along. Embrace challenges and setbacks as opportunities for growth, and don't be afraid to step outside your comfort zone and try new things.

Remember, success is not a destination, but rather a journey. So embrace the journey and enjoy the process of becoming the best version of yourself. You are truly an unstoppable force of nature, and with the right habits and mindset, nothing can stand in the way of your achieving your goals and reaching your full potential.

Chapter 1: Creating a vision for your life

Creating a vision for one's life is an essential step in the journey toward personal and professional success. Highly effective people understand that having a clear and inspiring vision provides direction, focus, and motivation, and helps them make better decisions, prioritize their efforts, and achieve their goals. Here are some tips on how highly effective people create a vision for their lives:

Define their values and priorities: Before creating a vision, highly effective people take the time to reflect on what is truly important to them and what they want to achieve in life. This helps them determine their values and priorities, which serve as the foundation for their vision.

Set specific and measurable goals: Highly effective people set specific and measurable goals that align with their values and priorities. These goals provide a roadmap for their vision and help them track their progress.

Imagine their future self: Highly effective people use visualization techniques to bring their vision to life. They imagine what their life will look like once they have achieved their goals and take time to focus on this image.

Write down their vision: Writing down their vision helps highly effective people clarify their thoughts and gives them a tangible reference to refer to in the future.

Review and adjust: Highly effective people regularly review and adjust their vision as needed to ensure it remains relevant and aligned with their values and priorities.

A friend of mine, Jack Capasso, once told me how he transformed from being a failure to a successful person.

Jack said he felt lost and unfulfilled in life moving from job to job, and never felt a sense of purpose.

One day, Jack said he decided to take some time to reflect on his life and figure out what he truly wanted. He realized that he had never taken the time to create a vision for his life.

So, Jack got to work. He sat down and thought about his passions, values, and what would bring him true happiness. He wrote down his goals and aspirations for the future, both short-term and long-term.

With his vision in mind, Jack was able to make small changes in his daily life that aligned with his newfound purpose. He started to focus on building his skills, making meaningful connections with others, and actively pursuing his goals.

As time passed, Jack began to see the fruits of his labor. He landed a job that he was passionate about and was surrounded by people who brought joy and positivity into his life. He was finally living the life he had envisioned for himself.

From that day forward, Jack never forgot the importance of having a clear vision for his life. He continued to work towards his goals and found fulfillment in every aspect of his life.

Creating a vision for one's life requires effort and commitment, but it is well worth it. By following these steps, highly effective people are able to focus their energy and resources on what matters most to them, ultimately leading to a more fulfilling and successful life.

Practical tips to create a vision for your life:

Start with self-reflection:
Take some time to reflect on what is important to you, what you value, and what you want to achieve in life. This will give you a good starting point for creating your vision.

Set clear and specific goals: Make sure your goals are specific, measurable, and attainable. Write them down and refer to them often to keep your vision in focus.

Prioritize your goals: Determine which goals are most important to you and prioritize them accordingly. Focus your time and energy on achieving the most important goals first.

Create a vision board: A vision board is a visual representation of your goals and aspirations. Cut out images and quotes that inspire you and paste them on a board or canvas. Place your vision board where you can see it every day to keep your vision at the forefront of your mind.

Surround yourself with positivity: Seek out positive people, environments, and experiences that align with your vision. Surrounding yourself with positivity will help you stay motivated and focused.

Take action: Creating a vision for your life is not enough; you must take action to make it a reality. Set achievable milestones and celebrate your successes along the way.

Stay flexible: Life is unpredictable and your vision may change as you go. Be open to adjusting your vision as you grow and evolve.

Remember, creating a vision for your life is a continuous process and requires consistent effort. Stay focused, stay positive, and trust the journey.

Please, permit me share a bit of my story here.

I was just an average person, with average talents and abilities. I didn't stand out in any particular area and was just going through life, doing what was expected of me. But that all changed when I discovered the power of habits and how they can shape our lives. I started small, focusing on developing good habits in one area of my life, and then gradually added more.

At first, it was challenging. Old habits die hard, and I found myself slipping back into my old ways at times. But I didn't give up. I reminded myself of my goal and pushed on. Slowly but surely, I started to see changes. I was more productive, more focused, and more energized. I felt like a new person.

As I continued to develop new habits, I started to see more and more improvements in my life. My relationships improved, my finances improved, and my health improved. And then, something unexpected happened. People started to take notice. They started to ask me how I was doing it. They were fascinated by the changes they saw in me, and wanted to know how they could do the same.

That's when I realized that I had a unique opportunity to share what I had learned with others. I started speaking at events, sharing my story and the habits that had transformed my life. And to my surprise, people were inspired. They were motivated by my story and wanted to know more. That's when I decided to write this book.

Through effective habits, I went from being average to becoming exceptional. And I want to show others that they can too. Anyone can achieve greatness if they have the right tools and the right mindset. That's what this book is all about. It's about sharing the habits that have transformed my life and showing others how they can do the same.

I've included all the tips, tricks, and strategies that I've learned along the way. I've included practical advice that anyone can implement, no matter where they are in their journey.

I hope that this book will motivate and inspire you to take action. I hope that it will help you see the incredible potential that lies within you. And I hope that it will show you that anything is possible if you have the right habits and the right mindset.

So if you're ready to take your life to the next level, then let's get to the next chapter and subsequent ones.

Together, we can achieve greatness.

Chapter 2: Prioritizing self-care and personal development

Self-care and personal development are two crucial aspects of life that are often neglected in the pursuit of success and productivity. However, highly effective people understand that prioritizing these areas leads to better overall well-being and performance. Here are a few reasons why:

Improved Mental Health: Regular self-care activities such as exercise, meditation, and adequate sleep help to reduce stress and improve mental health. A healthy mind is essential for optimal functioning and decision-making.

Enhanced Resilience: Personal development activities like learning new skills and practicing self-reflection can help build

resilience. Highly effective people are better equipped to handle challenging situations and bounce back from setbacks more quickly.

Increased Confidence and Self-Awareness: Prioritizing personal development can also lead to an increased understanding of oneself and one's values, which can enhance self-confidence and decision-making abilities.

Better Work-Life Balance: Self-care and personal development help individuals maintain a healthy work-life balance. This can lead to higher job satisfaction and improved relationships outside of work.

Prioritizing self-care and personal development requires intentional effort and a commitment to making it a priority. Here are some steps you can take:

Make a plan: Decide on specific goals for your self-care and personal development and make a plan for how you will achieve them.

Set aside time: Make time for self-care and personal development activities every day or week, and stick to it as you would any other appointment.

Eliminate distractions: Find ways to minimize or eliminate distractions that interfere with your self-care and personal development efforts.

Here are some practical strategies to help eliminate distractions that interfere with your self-care and personal development:

- Establish clear goals: Start by defining what you want to achieve in a day or week and prioritize tasks that align

  with those goals. This will help you stay focused on what's important.

- Create a designated workspace: If you work from home, create a specific space for work that is free from distractions such as noise, clutter, and interruptions.

- Turn off notifications: Silence your phone or turn off notifications for non-essential apps to minimize interruptions during work hours.

- Use time blocking: Schedule specific blocks of time for different tasks, and stick to the schedule as much as possible. This helps eliminate the temptation to switch between tasks and keeps you focused.

- Practice mindfulness: Mindfulness can help you become more aware of

- distractions and resist the urge to react to them. Try meditating, doing yoga, or simply taking deep breaths throughout the day.

- Take breaks: Regular breaks help refresh your mind and reduce burnout. Go for a walk, stretch, or do something you enjoy to help you refocus when you return to work.

By following these steps, you can eliminate distractions and increase your focus, productivity, and overall well-being.

Practice self-discipline: Stay committed to your self-care and personal development goals, even when it is difficult.

Seek support: Surround yourself with supportive people who understand and encourage your self-care and personal development efforts.

Stay motivated: Celebrate your progress and remind yourself why self-care and personal development are important to you.

Remember that prioritizing self-care and personal development is an ongoing process, and it may take time to see results. Stay committed, be patient, and celebrate your progress along the way.

In conclusion, highly effective people prioritize self-care and personal development because it leads to improved mental health, increased resilience, enhanced confidence, and better work-life balance. By taking the time to invest in themselves, they are better equipped to perform at their best and achieve their goals.

Chapter 3: Building healthy relationships

Building healthy relationships is a critical aspect of personal and professional success. Highly effective people understand the importance of fostering positive connections with others, and they work hard to maintain strong and meaningful relationships. In this chapter, we'll explore the key strategies that highly effective people use to build and maintain healthy relationships.

Communication: Communication is the cornerstone of all healthy relationships. Highly effective people make a point of actively listening to their friends, family, and colleagues. They avoid making assumptions and instead ask questions to clarify misunderstandings. They also express themselves clearly and concisely, avoiding passive-aggressive behavior and instead taking responsibility for their own emotions and thoughts.

Empathy: Empathy is the ability to understand and share the feelings of others. Highly effective people understand that relationships are about more than just getting what they want; they also want to make sure the other person is happy and fulfilled. By showing empathy, they can build strong bonds of trust and mutual understanding.

Honesty: Honesty is essential for building healthy relationships. Highly effective people are honest in their communication and avoid making promises they can't keep. They are transparent about their intentions and do not manipulate others for their own gain. This helps to build trust and strengthens relationships over time.

Active Listening: Active listening is a critical skill for building healthy relationships. Highly effective people listen attentively to what others are saying and show genuine interest in their concerns. They avoid interrupting and instead wait until the other person has finished speaking before offering their thoughts. This type of listening helps to build mutual respect and understanding, making it easier to resolve conflicts and maintain positive relationships.

Mutual Respect: Mutual respect is another key ingredient in healthy relationships. Highly effective people understand that every person has their own unique experiences and perspectives, and they respect these differences. They avoid judgment and instead show compassion and understanding. By showing respect for others, they create a positive and supportive environment where everyone feels valued.

Compromise: Compromise is an important aspect of building healthy relationships. Highly effective people understand that it is not always possible to get what they want, and they are willing to make compromises for the sake of the relationship. They also respect others' boundaries and avoid pushing their agendas at the expense of others.

Gratitude: Gratitude is a powerful tool for building healthy relationships. Highly effective people make a point of expressing gratitude for the positive things in their lives, including their relationships. They show appreciation for others' efforts and are thankful for the support and love they receive. By showing gratitude, they can strengthen bonds and create a positive and supportive environment.

Forgiveness: Forgiveness is an important aspect of building healthy relationships.

Highly effective people understand that mistakes are a natural part of life and that everyone is capable of making them. They are willing to forgive others, even when it is difficult, and avoid holding grudges. By letting go of negative feelings, they can move forward and maintain positive relationships.

Quality Time: Quality time is essential for building healthy relationships. Highly effective people make a point of spending time with those they care about, whether it be friends, family, or colleagues. They create meaningful experiences and enjoy spending time together, strengthening bonds, and building positive memories.

Support: Support is an important aspect of building healthy relationships. Highly effective people understand that relationships are about giving and receiving support. They offer encouragement and support to others, even when it is difficult, and seek support for themselves when needed. By providing and receiving support, they can build strong and meaningful relationships.

Building healthy relationships is a critical aspect of personal and professional success.

Building and maintaining healthy relationships is a vital aspect of our lives, and it can greatly impact our overall happiness and well-being. Relationships can come in many forms - romantic, familial, friendship, professional, and more. Regardless of the type of relationship, all healthy relationships have certain common characteristics that make them strong and fulfilling.

Here are some practical ways to build and maintain healthy relationships:

Communication is key in any relationship. It is important to be open and honest with one another and to actively listen to each other's thoughts and feelings. This means being willing to share your thoughts and feelings and being present and attentive when the other person is speaking.

Trust is essential in any relationship, and it is something that is built over time through consistency, honesty, and reliability. Trust can be damaged easily, but it can also be repaired through time, effort, and understanding.

Empathy involves understanding and being sensitive to others' emotions and experiences. When you can put yourself in another person's shoes, it helps to build a deeper and more meaningful connection.

In healthy relationships, both parties support one another in their goals, dreams, and challenges. This includes providing emotional support, encouragement, and being there for each other through good times and bad.

Relationships require flexibility and a willingness to adapt to change. This means being open to new ideas, new perspectives, and new ways of doing things. It also means being willing to compromise when necessary.

Building a relationship around shared interests and values can help to strengthen the bond between two people. This can help to create a sense of connection and make it easier to find common ground.

Spending quality time together is important in any relationship. This can involve doing things together, such as hobbies or interests, or simply spending time talking and being present with one another.

All healthy relationships are built on mutual respect. This means treating others with dignity and treating one another's feelings and opinions with consideration.

While it is important to be supportive of one another, it is also important for each person to maintain their independence and their sense of identity. This means having separate interests, friends, and goals, and not becoming overly dependent on one another.

Expressing gratitude and appreciation can help to build a strong and healthy relationship. This can involve simple acts of kindness, such as saying "thank you" and expressing genuine appreciation for one another.

In conclusion, building and maintaining healthy relationships require time, effort, and commitment. By focusing on communication, trust, empathy, support, flexibility, shared interests and values, quality time, respect, independence, and gratitude and appreciation, you can build strong and fulfilling relationships that will enhance your life. Remember that relationships are a two-way street, and it takes the effort of both parties to make them work.

Chapter 4: Developing a growth mindset

Developing a growth mindset is a crucial factor in becoming highly effective and successful.

A growth mindset is a belief that one's abilities and intelligence can be developed through effort, learning, and perseverance. In contrast, a fixed mindset is the belief that one's abilities and intelligence are set and cannot be changed. The difference between these two mindsets can have a significant impact on a person's life and their ability to achieve their goals.

People with a growth mindset embrace challenges, see failures as opportunities to learn and grow and persevere in the face of difficulties. They understand that their abilities and intelligence are not fixed and can be developed through hard work and dedication. On the other hand, people with a fixed mindset avoid challenges, see failures as evidence of their limitations, and give up easily when faced with difficulties.

Developing a growth mindset is a lifelong process that requires effort and commitment. Here are some strategies for developing a growth mindset:

Embrace challenges: People with a growth mindset embrace challenges as opportunities to learn and grow. They see challenges as a way to stretch their abilities and gain new skills. Embracing challenges helps you develop resilience and persistence, which are crucial for success.

Practice self-reflection: Regularly reflect on your thoughts, behaviors, and actions. Ask yourself questions such as, "What did I learn from this experience?" and "How can I use what I learned to improve in the future?" This practice helps you gain insights into your mindset and how it affects your life.

Seek feedback: Ask for feedback from others and be open to constructive criticism. Feedback provides valuable insights into areas where you can improve and grow.

Cultivate a growth-oriented environment: Surround yourself with people who support and encourage your growth. Seek mentors and surround yourself with like-minded individuals who have a growth mindset.

Embrace failure: People with a growth mindset view failure as an opportunity to learn and grow. They understand that failure is not a reflection of their worth or abilities, but a chance to try again and improve. Embracing failure helps you develop resilience and persistence, which are crucial for success.

Focus on the process, not just the outcome: People with a growth mindset focus on the process of learning and growing, rather than just the outcome. They understand that success is not a destination, but a journey. By focusing on the process, they stay motivated and committed to their goals.

Cultivate a positive attitude: People with a growth mindset maintain a positive attitude, even in the face of difficulties. They believe in their abilities and are confident that they can grow and develop. Cultivating a positive attitude helps you stay motivated and focused on your goals.

However, failing to develop a growth mindset can lead to several negative consequences. In this discussion, we will explore the consequences of failing to develop a growth mindset in greater detail.

Limited Achievement

One of the main consequences of a fixed mindset is a limited achievement. People with fixed mindsets believe that their abilities and intelligence are set, and they don't believe that they can improve. This can lead to a lack of effort and motivation, as they don't push themselves to learn and grow. For example, if someone with a fixed mindset believes that they are not naturally talented in a certain subject, they may give up on learning that subject, instead of putting in the effort to improve their abilities.

In contrast, people with a growth mindset are more likely to embrace challenges and push themselves to improve. They see failure as an opportunity to learn and grow, and they are motivated to work hard and overcome obstacles. This mindset leads to a greater willingness to take risks and try new things, which can result in greater personal and professional growth.

Fear of Failure

People with a fixed mindset often fear failure because they believe that it reflects on their abilities. This fear can lead to a lack of effort and risk-taking, which can hold them back from reaching their full potential. For example, someone with a fixed mindset may avoid trying out for a sports team or applying for a job that they believe they are not naturally talented at, because they don't want to fail and be seen as inadequate.

In contrast, people with a growth mindset see failure as a natural part of the learning process. They believe that failure is an opportunity to learn and grow, rather than a reflection of their abilities. This mindset leads to a greater willingness to take risks and try new things, even if the outcome is uncertain. This can lead to greater personal and professional growth and success, as people with a growth mindset are more likely to embrace challenges and overcome obstacles.

Lack of Resilience

Resilience is the ability to bounce back from adversity and maintain a positive outlook. People with fixed mindsets may struggle with resilience because they believe that they cannot change their abilities or traits. This can lead to a lack of effort and a negative outlook, as they may give up easily when faced with challenges or setbacks.

In contrast, people with a growth mindset are better equipped to handle challenges and setbacks because they believe that they can learn from their mistakes and grow from their experiences. This mindset leads to a greater willingness to embrace challenges and persist in the face of adversity, which can result in greater personal and professional growth.

Stifled Creativity

A growth mindset encourages creativity and innovation because it allows people to see failure as an opportunity to learn and grow, rather than a reflection of their abilities. People with a fixed mindset may avoid taking risks and trying new things because they don't want to fail. This can lead to a lack of creativity and innovation, as people are less likely to embrace new opportunities and experiences.

In contrast, people with a growth mindset are more likely to take risks and embrace new opportunities, even if they are uncertain of the outcome. This mindset leads to a greater willingness to try new things and explore new ideas, which can result in greater creativity and innovation.

Negative Impact on Relationships

A fixed mindset can also have a negative impact on relationships, as it can lead to a lack of trust and communication, as one partner may feel as though they are not being heard or understood. It can also lead to a fear of vulnerability and a lack of willingness to take risks, which can prevent partners from growing and evolving together.

Overall, having a fixed mindset can make it difficult for individuals to form and maintain healthy, fulfilling relationships. It's important to cultivate a growth mindset, which emphasizes the idea that abilities and characteristics can be developed and improved through effort and experience.

In conclusion, developing a growth mindset is essential for highly effective people. A growth mindset helps individuals embrace challenges, see failures as opportunities to learn and grow, and persevere in the face of difficulties. By embracing challenges, seeking feedback, focusing on the process, and cultivating a positive attitude, individuals can develop a growth mindset and achieve their goals.

REFLECT

Dear reader,

As you journey through the pages of this book, I encourage you to take a moment and reflect on the information you have just read. Consider the themes and messages that have been presented, and think about how they apply to your own life and experiences.

Allow yourself to contemplate the implications of the information and ideas contained within these pages. What insights have you gained? How might these insights change your perspective or shape your future actions?

Take a deep breath, clear your mind, and allow yourself to truly consider the impact of what you have just read. Your thoughts and reflections are valuable, so take the time to fully engage with the material before moving on.

Thank you for taking the time to reflect, and I hope you continue to enjoy the journey through this book.

Chapter 5: Cultivating a daily mindfulness practice

Highly effective people understand the importance of cultivating a daily mindfulness practice. Mindfulness refers to the act of being present in the moment and paying attention to one's thoughts, feelings, and surroundings without judgment. It has been proven to have numerous benefits including improved focus, reduced stress, increased self-awareness, and enhanced overall well-being.

Here are a few ways highly effective people cultivate a daily mindfulness practice:

Establish a routine: The first step to cultivating a daily mindfulness practice is to establish a routine. Highly effective people find a specific time each day to practice mindfulness, whether it's in the morning, during a lunch break, or before bed. They stick to this routine and make it a non-negotiable part of their daily schedule.

Start small: Mindfulness can be intimidating, especially for beginners. Highly effective people understand this and start small, setting aside just a few minutes each day to practice mindfulness. As they become more comfortable, they can gradually increase the amount of time they dedicate to mindfulness.

Practice mindfulness in various forms: There are many different forms of mindfulness, including meditation, deep breathing exercises, yoga, and even simple activities like taking a walk. Highly effective people try different forms of mindfulness and find what works best for them. They may also switch between forms depending on the day and their needs.

Use triggers: Highly effective people use triggers to remind themselves to be mindful throughout the day. This might be setting a phone reminder, putting a sticky note on their computer, or simply making a mental note to check in with themselves.

Embrace silence: One of the most powerful forms of mindfulness is simply being quiet and still. Highly effective people understand the importance of embracing silence and making time each day to sit quietly and reflect. They may use this time to meditate, journal, or simply be still.

Stay focused: The goal of mindfulness is to be present in the moment and not get lost in thoughts about the past or future. Highly effective people stay focused on their breath and the present moment, gently redirecting their thoughts when they wander.

Practice non-judgment: Mindfulness is about observing and accepting one's thoughts and feelings without judgment. Highly effective people practice non-judgment and recognize that all thoughts and emotions are valid.

Be consistent: Mindfulness is most effective when practiced consistently. Highly effective people make mindfulness a daily habit and don't let distractions or other responsibilities get in the way.

Use technology: There are many apps and websites available that can help with mindfulness.

Consider the following technology:

Meditation Apps: There are several meditation apps available that provide guided meditations and mindfulness exercises to help users reduce stress and increase focus. Some of these apps also have features like progress tracking, reminders, and personalized programs to make practicing mindfulness more accessible and engaging.

Wearables: Wearable technology, such as smartwatches and fitness trackers, can help track stress levels and offer mindfulness exercises to help users manage stress in real-time. These devices can also track physical activity, sleep patterns, and heart rate, providing a more holistic view of overall well-being.

Virtual Reality: Virtual reality technology is being used to create immersive mindfulness experiences, such as guided meditations in beautiful virtual environments. This can help users escape from distractions and focus on the present moment.

Smart Home Devices: Smart home devices, such as smart lights and sound systems, can be programmed to create an atmosphere conducive to mindfulness and relaxation. For example, a smart light system can automatically adjust lighting levels and color to create a calming environment, while a smart sound system can play soothing music or guided meditations.

Technology can be a helpful tool in promoting mindfulness, providing new and innovative ways to help individuals incorporate mindfulness into their daily lives.

Highly effective people use technology to support their daily practice and find resources that work best for them.

Make mindfulness a part of their daily life: Highly effective people don't just practice mindfulness for a few minutes each day;

they make it a part of their daily life. They approach every task and interaction with mindfulness, paying attention to their thoughts and feelings and staying present in the moment.

In conclusion, cultivating a daily mindfulness practice is a key component of the habits of highly effective people. By establishing a routine, starting small, practicing in various forms, using triggers, embracing silence, staying focused, practicing non-judgment, being consistent, using technology, and making mindfulness a part of their daily life, highly effective people reap the many benefits of mindfulness. Whether it's improved focus, reduced stress, increased self-awareness, or enhanced overall well-being, daily mindfulness practice is an investment in one's mental and emotional health.

Chapter 6: Establishing healthy habits and routines

Establishing healthy habits and routines is a key factor in achieving success and leading a fulfilling life. Highly effective people understand this and make it a priority to develop habits that support their well-being, productivity, and growth. In this chapter, we will explore some of the ways in which highly effective people establish healthy habits and routines and how you can adopt these strategies in your own life.

Start small: When it comes to developing new habits, starting small is crucial. It is important to set achievable goals that can be easily incorporated into your daily routine. For example, if your goal is to exercise every day, begin with a 10-minute workout and gradually increase the duration as you get stronger.

Make it a priority: Highly effective people understand that habits and routines require effort and discipline. They make it a priority to allocate time each day to focus on their goals and habits, no matter how busy they may be.

Plan ahead: Effective planning is essential to establishing healthy habits and routines. Highly effective people create detailed schedules that include time for exercise, self-care, and other important activities. They also make sure to schedule time for relaxation and self-reflection to maintain a healthy balance.

Stay consistent: Consistency is key when it comes to establishing healthy habits. Highly effective people understand that habits take time to form and that it is important to stay focused and dedicated to the process.

Celebrate your successes: Highly effective people understand the importance of recognizing and celebrating their successes, no matter how small they may be. This helps to keep them motivated and on track with their goals.

Create a supportive environment: Surrounding yourself with supportive and like-minded individuals can greatly increase your chances of success in establishing healthy habits and routines. Highly effective people seek out friends, family members, and colleagues who share their values and support their goals.

Track your progress: Keeping track of your progress is a great way to stay motivated and focused on your goals. Highly effective people track their habits and routines, monitoring their progress and making adjustments as necessary.

Be patient: Establishing healthy habits and routines takes time, and highly effective people understand that patience is key. They know that success comes from consistent effort and that it is important to give themselves time to adapt to new habits.

Why establishing healthy habits is hard

Establishing healthy habits and routines can be a challenging task for many people, and there are several reasons for this. We will explore the various factors that contribute to this difficulty and how individuals can overcome them to achieve their goals.

Lack of motivation and inspiration
One of the primary reasons why people struggle to establish healthy habits is a lack of motivation and inspiration. Establishing

healthy habits requires discipline and effort, and without a strong sense of why these habits are important, it can be difficult to maintain the motivation to stick to them. Furthermore, people may not feel inspired by their goals or the process of establishing healthy habits, making it difficult to stay engaged and motivated.

Busy lifestyles
Another significant factor that contributes to the difficulty of establishing healthy habits is a busy lifestyle. With work, family, and other commitments, it can be challenging to carve out time for self-care and healthy habits. People may feel overwhelmed by their schedule and feel like they simply don't have the time to make changes to their lifestyles.

Lack of accountability
Many people struggle with accountability when it comes to establishing healthy

habits. They may not have a support system in place that holds them accountable to their goals, making it easy to fall back into old patterns and habits. In some cases, people may not feel comfortable sharing their goals with others or may feel like they are being judged for their efforts.

Fear of failure
Fear of failure can also be a significant barrier to establishing healthy habits. People may be afraid of failing to meet their goals or of not being able to stick to their habits, which can lead to a lack of confidence and a decreased likelihood of making positive changes. This fear can be especially strong for people who have tried and failed to establish healthy habits in the past.

Unhealthy coping mechanisms
Some people may use unhealthy habits and behaviors as a way of coping with stress,

anxiety, or other life challenges. For these individuals, changing their habits may feel like they are giving up a source of comfort or support, making it difficult to establish healthy routines. In some cases, they may not recognize the negative impact that their habits are having on their well-being, making it challenging to make changes.

Lack of knowledge and resources
Another factor that can make it difficult to establish healthy habits is a lack of knowledge and resources. People may not know where to turn for information and guidance on how to establish healthy habits, or they may not have access to the resources and support that they need. This can make the process of establishing healthy habits feel overwhelming and unattainable.

Despite these challenges, there are strategies that individuals can use to overcome these barriers and establish healthy habits and routines. Here are some tips to help you get started:

Set clear and achievable goals
To establish healthy habits, it is essential to set clear and achievable goals. This will help you focus on what you want to accomplish and give you a sense of direction. When setting goals, it is important to be realistic about what you can achieve and to break down larger goals into smaller, manageable steps.

Find motivation and inspiration
To stay motivated and inspired, it is important to have a strong sense of why your goals are important to you. Take the time to reflect on what you want to achieve and what your values and priorities are. You can also seek out inspiration by connecting with others who have similar goals or by following role models who embody the habits and routines that you aspire to adopt.

Make time for self-care
Establishing healthy habits requires time and effort, so it is important to make time for self-care and prioritize your well-being.

In conclusion, establishing healthy habits and routines is a key factor in leading a fulfilling and successful life. By starting small, making it a priority, planning ahead, staying consistent, celebrating your successes, creating a supportive environment, tracking your progress, and being patient, you can adopt the strategies used by highly effective people to achieve your goals and lead a healthier, more productive life.

Chapter 7: Nurturing a sense of purpose and meaning

Highly effective people often have a strong sense of purpose and meaning in their lives, which drives them toward their goals and helps them stay motivated. Here are some ways that highly effective people nurture a sense of purpose and meaning:

Identifying their values and beliefs: People who have a strong sense of purpose often have a clear understanding of what they value and believe in. By exploring their values and beliefs, they can better understand what drives them and what kind of life they want to lead.

Setting meaningful goals: Effective people set goals that are aligned with their values and beliefs. By doing so, they ensure that their efforts are directed towards something that truly matters to them, giving their life a sense of meaning and purpose.

Engaging in activities that bring fulfillment: People who have a strong sense of purpose often engage in activities that bring them fulfillment and joy. This could be anything from volunteering, practicing a hobby, or pursuing a passion. When they are engaged in activities that bring them happiness, they feel more connected to their sense of purpose.

Building relationships that matter: Effective people understand the importance of having supportive and meaningful relationships in their lives. By building strong relationships with friends and family, they feel connected to others and find meaning in their interactions.

Reflecting on their life: People who have a strong sense of purpose often reflect on their life regularly. They take time to assess what they have accomplished and what they still hope to achieve. This self-reflection helps them stay aligned with their values and beliefs, and ensures that their actions are aligned with their sense of purpose.

Contributing to others: Effective people understand that their purpose is not just about themselves, but also about making a difference in the world. By contributing to others, they find meaning and fulfillment in their lives. This could be anything from volunteering, mentoring others, or simply being kind and compassionate to those around them.

Being grateful: People who have a strong sense of purpose are often grateful for what they have in their lives. By cultivating an attitude of gratitude, they are able to appreciate their blessings and find meaning in their life experiences.

In conclusion, highly effective people nurture a sense of purpose and meaning by understanding their values and beliefs, setting meaningful goals, engaging in activities that bring fulfillment, building relationships that matter, reflecting on their life, contributing to others, and being grateful. By doing so, they can lead a life that is fulfilling and meaningful.

Chapter 8: Embracing resilience and perseverance

Highly effective people are known for their ability to handle challenges and obstacles with grace, determination, and resilience. Embracing resilience and perseverance is a key factor in their success, allowing them to overcome adversity and turn setbacks into opportunities.

In this chapter, we'll explore what resilience and perseverance are, why they're important, and how highly effective people embrace them in their lives.

Resilience refers to the ability to bounce back from adversity and overcome challenges. It's a combination of personal attributes, such as mental toughness, positive outlook, and emotional intelligence, as well as supportive relationships and healthy coping mechanisms. Resilient people can adapt to change and handle stress with ease, which helps them overcome obstacles and achieve their goals.

Perseverance, on the other hand, is the quality of continuing to work hard or stay determined despite difficulties, obstacles, or setbacks. It is the ability to keep going and not give up, even when faced with challenges and failures.

Perseverance is an important trait for achieving goals and success in life, as it allows individuals to keep pushing forward and overcome adversity. It requires determination, resilience, and a positive attitude.

Having perseverance means having the courage to face challenges head-on and the ability to learn from failures and turn them into opportunities for growth and development.

There are several obstacles one may face when embracing resilience and perseverance, and some of these include:

Negative thoughts and self-doubt: Negative thoughts and self-doubt can erode confidence and make it difficult to bounce back from setbacks.

Lack of support: Lack of support from friends, family, and colleagues can make it challenging to persevere in the face of adversity.

Burnout: Trying to do too much and pushing oneself too hard can lead to burnout and make it difficult to maintain a resilient and persevering mindset.

Overwhelm: Feeling overwhelmed by the demands of work, relationships, and other responsibilities can make it difficult to stay focused and motivated.

However, these obstacles can be overcome by taking the following steps:

Cultivate a growth mindset: Focus on learning from setbacks and failures, and view challenges as opportunities for growth.

Seek support: Surround yourself with positive, supportive people who believe in your abilities and encourage you to keep going.

Practice self-care: Prioritize self-care activities, such as exercise, meditation, and spending time with loved ones, to prevent burnout and maintain your resilience.

Set realistic goals: Break down large, overwhelming tasks into smaller, manageable steps and set realistic goals to avoid feeling overwhelmed.

Maintain a positive attitude: Stay focused on the positive aspects of life and maintain a positive outlook, even in the face of adversity.

Yes, resilience is indeed an important aspect of achieving success. Resilience is the ability to bounce back from setbacks and challenges, and it is a critical trait for anyone who wants to reach their goals.

Success often requires perseverance, determination, and the ability to keep going despite obstacles and difficulties.

Resilient people can stay focused on their goals, even when things get tough, and they are better equipped to handle the ups and downs that come with the pursuit of success. By being resilient, individuals can not only overcome obstacles but also grow and learn from their experiences, which can help them become even more successful in the long run.

The qualities of resilience and perseverance are important for success and growth both personally and professionally.

In life, there will always be challenges and difficulties, but it's how one responds to those challenges that can make all the difference. By embracing resilience and perseverance, individuals can develop a growth mindset, which can help them overcome obstacles and reach their goals.

Developing resilience and perseverance requires a combination of personal qualities such as determination, a positive attitude, and a willingness to learn from failures.

Again, practicing self-care, staying positive, and setting realistic goals can also help individuals maintain their resilience and perseverance in the face of challenges.

In conclusion, embracing resilience and perseverance is essential for personal and professional growth, and can help individuals overcome challenges and achieve their goals.

Chapter 9: Fostering a culture of gratitude and positivity

Gratitude and positivity are two important aspects of a healthy and fulfilling life. A culture of gratitude and positivity can enhance an individual's well-being, improve relationships, and increase job satisfaction.

Despite these benefits, fostering a culture of gratitude and positivity can be a challenging task in today's fast-paced, ever-changing world. In this discussion, we will explore the difficulties in creating and maintaining a culture of gratitude and positivity.

One of the difficulties in fostering a culture of gratitude and positivity is the prevalence of negativity in society. Negative news, criticism, and complaints are often more attention-grabbing and memorable than positive news, praise, and compliments. This constant barrage of negativity can lead to a negative outlook and make it difficult to focus on the positive aspects of life.

In addition, social media and other forms of technology have made it easier for negativity to spread and amplify. As a result, it can be challenging to maintain a positive outlook and cultivate a culture of gratitude when negativity is so prevalent.

Another difficulty in fostering a culture of gratitude and positivity is the fast-paced and constantly changing nature of our lives.

With the demands of work, family, and other responsibilities, it can be difficult to take time to reflect on the things we are grateful for and appreciate the positive aspects of our lives. We often feel like we are just trying to keep up with the demands of daily life, leaving little time for reflection and gratitude.

In addition, the pace of change in the world can lead to feelings of uncertainty and instability, making it difficult to focus on the positive aspects of our lives.

The demands of modern life can also lead to feelings of burnout and exhaustion, making it difficult to maintain a positive outlook.

In our fast-paced world, it is common to work long hours, have multiple commitments, and be constantly connected to technology. This can lead to feelings of overwhelm and stress, making it challenging to focus on the things we are grateful for.

Also, feelings of burnout can make it difficult to maintain a positive outlook and a culture of gratitude.

Another difficulty in fostering a culture of gratitude and positivity is the impact of negative emotions. Negative emotions such as anger, frustration, and sadness can be overwhelming and can dominate our thoughts and actions. This can make it difficult to focus on the positive aspects of life and cultivate a culture of gratitude. In addition, negative emotions can be contagious, leading to a negative spiral of negativity that can be difficult to break out of.

It can be challenging to cultivate a culture of gratitude and positivity in an individualistic society. In many cultures, there is a focus on individual achievement and success, with little emphasis on community and interdependence. This individualistic focus can make it difficult to recognize and appreciate the contributions of others, leading to feelings of competition and resentment. In addition, it can be challenging to foster a culture of gratitude and positivity in a society where materialism and consumerism are highly valued.

Of truth, fostering a culture of gratitude and positivity in an ever-changing world can be challenging due to the prevalence of negativity, the fast-paced and constantly changing nature of our lives, feelings of burnout and exhaustion, the impact of negative emotions, and the individualistic focus of our society.

Despite these difficulties, it is important to focus on the positive aspects of our lives and cultivate a culture of gratitude and positivity for the benefit of our well-being and relationships. This can be achieved by taking time to reflect on the things we are grateful for and practicing gratitude and positive thinking.

In the midst of all these, we can learn from

highly effective people. They foster a culture of gratitude and positivity by adopting a number of habits and practices. Some of these include:

Practicing mindfulness: They take time to appreciate the present moment, rather than dwelling on the past or worrying about the future. This helps them stay focused on what they're grateful for, even in challenging circumstances.

Keeping a gratitude journal: They write down the things they're thankful for each day, which helps them cultivate an attitude of gratitude and positive thinking.

Surrounding themselves with positive people: They choose to spend time with people who are positive and supportive, rather than those who are negative or toxic.

Being intentional about positivity: They actively seek out opportunities to be positive

and spread joy to others, rather than waiting for positivity to come to them.

Focusing on what they can control: They understand that they can't control everything, but they can control their thoughts and actions. They focus on what they can do to make a positive impact, rather than dwelling on things they can't control.

Giving back to others: They understand that helping others is a great way to foster gratitude and positivity. Whether it's volunteering, donating, or simply spreading joy to those around them, they find ways to give back to others.

Staying optimistic: They have a positive outlook on life and see the glass as half full, rather than half empty. This helps them find the silver lining in even the most challenging situations.

By adopting these habits and practices, highly effective people can cultivate a culture of gratitude and positivity, even amidst all odds.

REFLECT

Again, how are you doing dear reader?

I hope you are enjoying the book so far and finding it helpful. If you are not feeling the impact of what you have learned so far, I encourage you to take a break and reflect on what you have read. It is important to remember that reading and understanding the material is just the first step. To truly make the most of the book and see the impact of its teachings, you need to put what you have learned into practice.

Take some time to think about how you can apply the concepts and ideas presented in the book to your own life and work. Try out new strategies, techniques, and approaches. Remember, knowledge without action is useless, so be proactive in your efforts to make the most of what you have learned.

If you find that you are struggling to make an impact with what you have learned so far, don't hesitate to reach out to others for support. Share your insights and experiences with friends, family, or colleagues who are also interested in the subject. Seek out additional resources or educational opportunities to deepen your understanding.

Keep in mind that the impact of a book is not always immediate and sometimes it takes time to see the results. However, with persistence and dedication, you can make a positive change in your life by putting into practice what you have learned so far.

Good luck!

Chapter 10: Developing effective communication skills

Effective communication is a crucial component of success, both professionally and personally. Highly effective people have a strong understanding of the importance of communication skills, and they invest time and effort into developing these skills.

One of the key elements of effective communication is the ability to listen actively. Listening actively involves paying close attention to the speaker, asking questions, and providing feedback. This type of listening allows the speaker to feel heard and understood, and it fosters an environment of trust and collaboration.

Another important aspect of effective communication is the ability to articulate thoughts and ideas clearly. This requires a strong understanding of language and the ability to express oneself in a way that is easy to understand. Highly effective people are often able to use simple, concise language to convey complex ideas, making it easier for their audience to grasp the message.

Developing strong communication skills is also important to understand the audience. This means considering factors such as age, culture, education level, and language preferences, and adapting one's communication style to meet the needs of the audience.

To engage an audience in communication skills, you can try the following:

Start with a hook: Begin with an interesting statement, a story, or a question to grab their attention.

Know your audience: Research and understand the background, interests, and needs of the audience. This will help you to tailor your message to their specific needs.

Be clear and concise: Speak clearly and use simple language that everyone can understand. Avoid using technical jargon unless you are sure that the audience is familiar with it.

Use visual aids: Use images, videos, and other visual aids to support your message and help keep the audience engaged.

Encourage participation: Ask questions, conduct polls, or involve the audience in activities to keep them involved and focused.

Show enthusiasm: Show genuine interest and enthusiasm for your topic. This will help to engage and motivate the audience.

End with a strong conclusion: Summarize your key points and leave a lasting impression on the audience by ending with a memorable statement or a call to action.

Highly effective people also understand the importance of body language in communication. They can use nonverbal cues, such as eye contact, facial expressions, and gestures, to enhance their message and build rapport with others.

Effective communication also requires the ability to manage conflict and navigate challenging conversations. Highly effective people can stay calm and composed in the face of disagreement, and they are skilled at finding common ground and constructively resolving conflicts.

Finally, highly effective people understand the value of feedback and continuous improvement. They seek out constructive feedback, and they use this feedback to continuously refine their communication skills and become even more effective communicators.

In conclusion, effective communication is a critical component of success, and highly effective people invest time and effort into developing strong communication skills. These skills include active listening, clear articulation, understanding the audience, utilizing body language, managing conflict, and seeking out feedback. By developing these skills, individuals can become highly effective communicators and achieve their personal and professional goals.

Chapter 11: Building a supportive community

Building a supportive community is a crucial aspect of personal and professional development. A supportive community is a group of individuals who offer encouragement, motivation, and resources to help you achieve your goals. In this article, we will explore the benefits of having a supportive community, the traits of highly effective people, and how to build a supportive community of your own.

Benefits of a Supportive Community

A supportive community provides a range of benefits that can help you achieve success in your personal and professional life. Some of the benefits of having a supportive community include:

Emotional support: A supportive community provides emotional support during difficult times. When you're facing challenges, a supportive community can offer encouragement and provide a shoulder to lean on.

Increased motivation: Being part of a supportive community can increase your motivation to achieve your goals. When you have a group of people cheering you on, you'll be more motivated to succeed.

Access to resources: A supportive community can provide access to valuable resources, such as information, contacts, and opportunities. This can help you overcome obstacles and achieve your goals faster.

Personal growth: A supportive community can help you grow as a person. You'll be exposed to different perspectives and ideas, which can help you expand your horizons and grow as a person.

Increased self-confidence: When you're part of a supportive community, you'll feel more confident in your abilities. This can help you take on new challenges and achieve your goals with greater ease.

Traits of Highly Effective People

Highly effective people are individuals who have achieved success in their personal and professional lives. These individuals have developed a set of traits that help them achieve their goals and live fulfilling lives. Some of the traits of highly effective people include:

Positive attitude: Highly effective people have a positive attitude, which helps them stay motivated and overcome obstacles.

Strong work ethic: Highly effective people have a strong work ethic, which helps them achieve their goals and maintain a high level of productivity.

Goal-oriented: Highly effective people are goal-oriented and have a clear understanding of what they want to achieve.

Self-discipline: Highly effective people have self-discipline, which helps them stay focused on their goals and avoid distractions.

Effective communication skills: Highly effective people have strong communication skills, which allows them to build strong relationships with others.

Building a Supportive Community

Building a supportive community can be a challenging task, but it is worth the effort.

Here are some steps to help you build a supportive community of your own:

Identify your goals: Start by identifying your goals and the areas of your life where you need support. This will help you determine what kind of support you need from your community.

Network: Networking is a crucial aspect of building a supportive community. Attend events and meet new people who share your interests and goals. You can also join clubs, organizations, or groups that are related to your goals.

Get involved: Get involved in your community by volunteering or participating in events. This will help you build relationships with others and create a sense of belonging.

Be a positive influence: Be a positive influence in your community by offering support and encouragement to others. This will help you build strong relationships with others and create a supportive atmosphere.

Share your experiences: Sharing your experiences with others can help build trust and create a sense of community. This can help you build strong relationships with others and receive support when you need it.

Chapter 12: Setting and achieving meaningful goals

Setting and achieving meaningful goals is a critical aspect of success for highly effective people. It is a key factor that distinguishes individuals who live a fulfilling life from those who just exist. By having a clear direction, highly effective people can make the most of their time, resources, and opportunities to create a life that is meaningful and fulfilling. In this article, we will explore the key principles and strategies that highly effective people use to set and achieve meaningful goals.

The first step in setting and achieving meaningful goals is to have a clear understanding of what is important to you. This requires taking the time to reflect on your values, passions, and aspirations. Once you have a clear understanding of what is important to you, it is easier to set goals that are aligned with your values and that truly matter to you.

The next step is to set specific, measurable, and achievable goals. Highly effective people understand that having a clear target makes it easier to stay motivated and focused. It also makes it easier to track progress and celebrate successes along the way. When setting goals, it is important to ensure that they are specific, measurable, and achievable. This means that the goal should be clear, concise, and well-defined. For example, instead of setting a goal to "improve your health," a specific and measurable goal would be "to lose 10 pounds in the next six months."

Highly effective people also understand the importance of setting deadlines for their goals. This creates a sense of urgency and helps to keep you focused and motivated. Deadlines also make it easier to track progress and determine if you are on track to achieve your goal.

In addition to setting specific, measurable, and achievable goals, highly effective people also understand the importance of having a plan. This means having a clear roadmap for how you are going to achieve your goals. This could include steps such as identifying the resources you need, breaking down the goal into smaller and more manageable tasks and creating a timeline for completion.

Another key aspect of setting and achieving meaningful goals is to have accountability. Highly effective people understand that having accountability helps to keep them focused and motivated. This could mean working with a coach or mentor, sharing your goals with a friend or family member, or keeping a journal of your progress.

Whatever method you choose, having accountability helps to keep you on track and to stay motivated.

Finally, highly effective people understand the importance of celebrating their successes. This means taking the time to acknowledge and celebrate the progress that they have made toward their goals. Celebrating successes helps to boost motivation, build confidence and reinforce the importance of setting and achieving meaningful goals.

Setting and achieving meaningful goals is a key aspect of success for highly effective people. By having a clear understanding of what is important to them, setting specific, measurable, and achievable goals, having a plan, having accountability, and celebrating their successes, highly effective people can create a life that is fulfilling and meaningful. By adopting these principles and strategies, anyone can become highly effective and achieve their goals.

"Believe in yourself and never give up on your dreams. The word 'impossible' only exists in the minds of those who lack the courage and determination to turn their visions into reality. You are capable of achieving great things, so trust your instincts, work hard, and stay focused on your goals. Remember, with determination, effort and perseverance, you can turn the impossible into the possible."

Chapter 13: Day-to-Day Life of Effective People

Highly effective individuals have a well-structured and disciplined daily routine that enables them to achieve their goals and lead fulfilling life.

They start their day early, usually with physical activity such as exercise or meditation, to energize their body and mind. They prioritize their tasks and have a to-do list, which helps them to stay focused and avoid wasting time on unimportant tasks. They prioritize their work, giving attention to the most critical tasks and delegating the rest, if necessary.

They are proactive in their approach and make the most of their time by avoiding distractions and procrastination. They communicate effectively, both in their personal and professional lives, and make sure to listen to others' perspectives. They also take time for self-care and engage in activities that bring them joy and relaxation, such as reading, traveling, or spending time with loved ones.

Highly effective individuals are also lifelong learners and continually work on personal growth. They invest in their education and professional development and seek out new knowledge and experiences that can help them improve. They maintain a positive attitude and keep their focus on their goals, even when faced with challenges. They are resilient and know how to bounce back from setbacks and failures.

Highly effective individuals lead a well-balanced life, making sure to prioritize their work and personal growth while also taking time for self-care and relaxation.

Their disciplined approach, proactive attitude, and focus on continuous improvement set them apart and enable them to achieve great things in their personal and professional lives.

It's important to note that everyone has different levels of productivity and what may be considered "less productive" for one person may not be the same for another. However, in general, people who are considered less productive may struggle to accomplish tasks, set and achieve goals, and manage their time effectively.

Some common traits of individuals with lower productivity levels include:

Procrastination: They may struggle to start tasks and often find themselves putting things off until the last minute.

Distractedness: They may have a hard time focusing and staying on track, often finding themselves getting sidetracked by other tasks or activities.

Lack of organization: They may have a disorganized workspace, cluttered to-do lists, and a general difficulty in keeping track of what needs to be done.

Poor time management: They may struggle to manage their time effectively, often spending too much time on non-essential tasks and not enough time on important ones.

Negative self-talk: They may have a tendency to focus on their shortcomings and engage in negative self-talk, which can further reduce their motivation and productivity.

However, it's important to remember that these traits can be changed with effort and determination. With the right strategies and tools, anyone can work to improve their productivity and lead a more fulfilling life.

Chapter 14: Twelve things highly effective people don't waste their time on and why

Success and effectiveness are traits that many people strive to attain in their personal and professional lives. However, it can often be difficult to determine what sets highly effective individuals apart from the rest. One key factor is the way they manage their time. By avoiding activities that waste time and energy, highly effective people can stay focused on their goals and maximize their productivity.

In this chapter, we will explore 12 things that highly effective people do not waste their time on, and why they are important for success. From avoiding negativity and drama to prioritizing their tasks and avoiding self-doubt, this chapter provides valuable insights into things highly effective individuals don't waste their time on.

Negativity and drama - Highly effective people understand that negativity and drama only drain their energy and distract them from their goals. They choose to surround themselves with positive, solution-focused individuals and avoid toxic environments.

Complaining - Complaining is a form of negativity that serves no purpose. Instead of complaining, highly effective people take action to find solutions to problems or seek out positive experiences.

Overthinking - Overthinking can lead to analysis paralysis, causing a person to waste time and not take action. Highly effective people have the ability to make quick, informed decisions and trust their instincts.

Time-wasting activities - Highly effective people are mindful of how they spend their time and actively avoid activities that do not bring value to their lives. This includes activities like excessive social media usage, watching too much television, or engaging in aimless conversation.

Perfectionism - Perfectionism can lead to endless revisions and delays, ultimately wasting time. Highly effective people understand that done is better than perfect and they take action to get their ideas out into the world.

Procrastination - Procrastination is a form of self-sabotage that prevents individuals from reaching their full potential. Highly effective people prioritize their tasks and work on them in a timely manner, avoiding the pitfalls of procrastination.

Unhealthy relationships - Relationships, whether personal or professional, can be time-consuming and emotionally draining. Highly effective people surround themselves with positive, supportive individuals and end unhealthy relationships that hold them back.

Fear of failure - Fear of failure can prevent individuals from taking risks and trying new things. Highly effective people embrace failure as an opportunity for growth and do not waste time being afraid to take action.

Holding grudges - Holding grudges takes up mental and emotional energy, preventing individuals from moving forward. Highly effective people choose to forgive and let go of grudges, freeing up their time and energy for more positive pursuits.

Self-doubt - Self-doubt can hold individuals back and prevent them from reaching their full potential. Highly effective people believe in themselves and their abilities, and they do not waste time on self-doubt.

Inefficient processes - Highly effective people are efficient in all aspects of their lives, including their work processes. They continuously evaluate and streamline their processes to avoid wasting time on inefficient practices.

Multitasking - Multitasking has been shown to decrease productivity and can lead to burnout. Highly effective people prioritize their tasks and focus on one thing at a time, avoiding the distractions and inefficiencies of multitasking.

Highly effective people understand the value of their time and actively avoid activities that do not bring value to their lives. They prioritize their tasks, surround themselves with positive individuals, and do not let negativity or self-doubt hold them back. By avoiding these 12 time-wasting activities, highly effective individuals can maximize their productivity and reach their full potential.

Summary

Developing effective habits is a key part of personal growth and can help you achieve your goals and live a more fulfilling life. Here are some tips to help you master the art of forming habits:

Start small: Habits take time to form, so it's important to start with something small and manageable. Focus on one habit at a time and make sure it becomes a part of your routine before moving on to the next.

Make it specific: Be clear about what you want to achieve and what the habit entails. For example, instead of simply saying "I want to exercise more," say "I want to go for a 30-minute walk every day at 5 PM."

Set a trigger: Habits are easier to stick to when they are triggered by a specific cue. For example, if you want to start reading before bed, place a book on your nightstand.

Track your progress: Keeping a record of your progress can help you stay motivated and on track. You can use a journal, a habit tracker app, or simply check off the days you have successfully completed the habit.

Celebrate successes: Celebrating small wins along the way can help keep you motivated and build momentum. Whether it's a pat on the back, a small treat, or simply acknowledging your progress, take the time to celebrate your successes.

Be patient: Habits take time to form, and it's normal to have setbacks along the way. Don't give up if you slip up – just get back on track as soon as possible.

Make it enjoyable: If you don't enjoy the habit, it will be difficult to stick to it in the long run. Find ways to make the habit more enjoyable, such as finding a workout partner, listening to music while exercising, or finding a new book to read.

Find accountability: Having someone hold you accountable can be a powerful motivator. Find a friend, family member, or coach to support you on your journey.

By following these tips and being consistent, you can master the art of forming effective habits and achieving your goals.

Remember, habits can play a significant role in personal growth and development. By incorporating positive habits into your daily routine, you can gradually improve various aspects of your life, such as your health, relationships, and career.

Here are some tips for harnessing the power of habits for personal growth:

Identify your goals: Start by figuring out what you want to achieve in different areas of your life. This could be anything from getting in shape to building stronger relationships with loved ones.

Create a plan: Once you know what you want to achieve, create a plan for how you will achieve it. This could involve setting specific goals, creating a schedule, and determining what habits you need to adopt to reach your goals.

Start small: When starting a new habit, it's important to start small. This makes it easier to stick to the habit and gradually build it into a larger part of your routine.

Track your progress: Keeping track of your progress can be a great motivator. You can use a journal, app, or spreadsheet to record your progress and see how far you've come.

Reward yourself: Celebrating small victories along the way can help keep you motivated. Set up a reward system for yourself and enjoy the rewards as you hit your milestones.

Be consistent: Consistency is key when it comes to forming new habits. Stick to your routine, even on days when you don't feel like it, and soon it will become second nature.

Surround yourself with support: Having a support system can make all the difference when it comes to adopting new habits. Surround yourself with people who encourage and support you, and reach out to them when you need help staying on track.

Congratulations on completing this book on effective habits! Reading is a powerful tool for self-improvement and personal growth, and by investing time and effort in this book, you have taken a significant step towards developing a more fulfilling and successful life.

The habits you have learned about can have a profound impact on every aspect of your life, from your health and relationships, to your career and overall happiness. So, keep up the good work and make these habits a part of your daily routine.

Remember, change takes time, but with perseverance and dedication, you can achieve your goals and live the life you desire.

Keep striving for excellence and never stop learning!

www.ingramcontent.com/pod-product-compliance
Lightning Source LLC
Chambersburg PA
CBHW071137220526
45467CB00015B/1293